MW01232850

MEDITERRANEAN DIET RECIPES VOL. 1

Delicious Mediterranean Meals to Lose
Weight with Taste

Sheryl Smith

Table of Contents

1. Artichoke Flatbread

✓ **Preparation time:** 10 minutes
✓ **Cooking time:** 15 minutes
✓ **Servings:** 4
✓ **Ingredients:**

- 5 tablespoons olive oil
- 2 garlic cloves, minced
- 2 tablespoons parsley, chopped
- 2 round whole wheat flatbreads
- 4 tablespoons parmesan, grated
- ½ cup mozzarella cheese, grated
- 14 ounces canned artichokes, drained and quartered
- 1 cup baby spinach, chopped
- ½ cup cherry tomatoes, halved
- ½ teaspoon basil, dried
- Salt and black pepper to the taste

Directions:

In a bowl, mix the parsley with the garlic and 4 tablespoons oil, whisk well and spread this over the flatbreads.

Sprinkle the mozzarella and half of the parmesan.

In a bowl, mix the artichokes with the spinach, tomatoes, basil, salt, pepper and the rest of the oil, toss and divide over the flatbreads as well.

Sprinkle the rest of the parmesan on top, arrange the flatbreads on a baking sheet lined with parchment paper and bake at 425 degrees F for 15 minutes.

Serve as an appetizer.

Nutrition: calories 223, fat 11.2, fiber 5.34, carbs 15.5, protein 7.4

2. Bulgur Lamb Meatballs

✓ **Preparation time:** 10 minutes

✓ **Cooking time:** 15 minutes

✓ **Servings:** 6

✓ **Ingredients:**

- 1 and ½ cups Greek yogurt
- ½ teaspoon cumin, ground
- 1 cup cucumber, shredded
- ½ teaspoon garlic, minced
- A pinch of salt and black pepper
- 1 cup bulgur
- 2 cups water
- 1 pound lamb, ground
- ¼ cup parsley, chopped
- ¼ cup shallots, chopped
- ½ teaspoon allspice, ground
- ½ teaspoon cinnamon powder
- 1 tablespoon olive oil

Directions:

In a bowl, combine the bulgur with the water, cover the bowl, leave aside for 10 minutes, drain and transfer to a bowl.

Add the meat, the yogurt and the rest of the ingredients except the oil, stir well and shape medium meatballs out of this mix.

Heat up a pan with the oil over medium-high heat, add the meatballs, cook them for 7 minutes on each side, arrange them all on a platter and serve as an appetizer.

Nutrition: calories 300, fat 9.6, fiber 4.6, carbs 22.6, protein 6.6

3. Chickpeas Salsa

✓ **Preparation time:** 5 minutes
✓ **Cooking time:** 0 minutes
✓ **Servings:** 6
✓ **Ingredients:**

- 4 spring onions, chopped
- 1 cup baby spinach
- 15 ounces canned chickpeas, drained and rinsed
- Salt and black pepper to the taste
- 2 tablespoons olive oil
- 2 tablespoons lemon juice
- 1 tablespoon cilantro, chopped

Directions:

In a bowl, mix the chickpeas with the spinach, spring onions and the rest of the ingredients, toss, divide into small cups and serve as a snack.

Nutrition: calories 224, fat 5.1, fiber 1, carbs 9.9, protein 15.1

5. Avocado Dip

✓ **Preparation time:** 5 minutes

✓ **Cooking time:** 0 minutes

✓ **Servings:** 8

✓ **Ingredients:**

- ½ cup heavy cream
- 1 green chili pepper, chopped
- Salt and pepper to the taste
- 4 avocados, pitted, peeled and chopped
- 1 cup cilantro, chopped
- ¼ cup lime juice

Directions:

In a blender, combine the cream with the avocados and the rest of the ingredients and pulse well.

Divide the mix into bowls and serve cold as a party dip.

Nutrition: calories 200, fat 14.5, fiber 3.8, carbs 8.1, protein 7.6

6. Chili Mango and Watermelon Salsa

✓ **Preparation time:** 5 minutes
✓ **Cooking time:** 0 minutes
✓ **Servings:** 12
✓ **Ingredients:**

- 1 red tomato, chopped
- Salt and black pepper to the taste
- 1 cup watermelon, seedless, peeled and cubed
- 1 red onion, chopped
- 2 mangos, peeled and chopped
- 2 chili peppers, chopped
- ¼ cup cilantro, chopped
- 3 tablespoons lime juice
- Pita chips for serving

Directions:

In a bowl, mix the tomato with the watermelon, the onion and the rest of the ingredients except the pita chips and toss well.

Divide the mix into small cups and serve with pita chips on the side.

Nutrition: calories 62, fat 4.7, fiber 1.3, carbs 3.9, protein 2.3

7. Coriander Falafel

✓ **Preparation time:** 10 minutes
✓ **Cooking time:** 10 minutes
✓ **Servings:** 8
✓ **Ingredients:**

- 1 cup canned garbanzo beans, drained and rinsed
- 1 bunch parsley leaves
- 1 yellow onion, chopped
- 5 garlic cloves, minced
- 1 teaspoon coriander, ground
- A pinch of salt and black pepper
- ¼ teaspoon cayenne pepper
- ¼ teaspoon baking soda
- ¼ teaspoon cumin powder
- 1 teaspoon lemon juice
- 3 tablespoons tapioca flour
- Olive oil for frying

Directions:

In your food processor, combine the beans with the parsley, onion and the rest the ingredients except the oil and the flour and pulse well.

Transfer the mix to a bowl, add the flour, stir well, shape 16 balls out of this mix and flatten them a bit.

Heat up a pan with some oil over medium-high heat, add the falafels, cook them for 5 minutes on each side, transfer to paper towels, drain excess grease, arrange them on a platter and serve as an appetizer.

Nutrition: calories 112, fat 6.2, fiber 2, carbs 12.3, protein 3.1

8. Creamy Spinach and Shallots Dip

✓ **Preparation time:** 10 minutes

✓ **Cooking time:** 0 minutes

✓ **Servings:** 4

✓ **Ingredients:**

- 1 pound spinach, roughly chopped
- 2 shallots, chopped
- 2 tablespoons mint, chopped
- ¾ cup cream cheese, soft
- Salt and black pepper to the taste

Directions:

In a blender, combine the spinach with the shallots and the rest of the ingredients, and pulse well.

Divide into small bowls and serve as a party dip.

Nutrition: calories 204, fat 11.5, fiber 3.1, carbs 4.2, protein 5.9

9. Cucumber Bites

✓ **Preparation time:** 10 minutes
✓ **Cooking time:** 0 minutes
✓ **Servings:** 12
✓ **Ingredients:**

- 1 English cucumber, sliced into 32 rounds
- 10 ounces hummus
- 16 cherry tomatoes, halved
- 1 tablespoon parsley, chopped
- 1 ounce feta cheese, crumbled

Directions:

Spread the hummus on each cucumber round, divide the tomato halves on each, sprinkle the cheese and parsley on to and serve as an appetizer.

Nutrition: calories 162, fat 3.4, fiber 2, carbs 6.4, protein 2.4

10.   Cucumber Rolls

✓ **Preparation time:** 5 minutes

✓ **Cooking time:** 0 minutes

✓ **Servings:** 6

✓ **Ingredients:**

- 1 big cucumber, sliced lengthwise
- 1 tablespoon parsley, chopped
- 8 ounces canned tuna, drained and mashed
- Salt and black pepper to the taste
- 1 teaspoon lime juice

Directions:

Arrange cucumber slices on a working surface, divide the rest of the ingredients, and roll.

Arrange all the rolls on a platter and serve as an appetizer.

Nutrition: calories 200, fat 6, fiber 3.4, carbs 7.6, protein 3.5

11. Cucumber Sandwich Bites

✓ **Preparation time:** 5 minutes

✓ **Cooking time:** 0 minutes

✓ **Servings:** 12

✓ **Ingredients:**

- 1 cucumber, sliced
- 8 slices whole wheat bread
- 2 tablespoons cream cheese, soft
- 1 tablespoon chives, chopped
- ¼ cup avocado, peeled, pitted and mashed
- 1 teaspoon mustard
- Salt and black pepper to the taste

Directions:

Spread the mashed avocado on each bread slice, also spread the rest of the ingredients except the cucumber slices.

Divide the cucumber slices on the bread slices, cut each slice in thirds, arrange on a platter and serve as an appetizer.

Nutrition: calories 187, fat 12.4, fiber 2.1, carbs 4.5, protein 8.2

12.   Eggplant Dip

✓ **Preparation time:** 10 minutes
✓ **Cooking time:** 40 minutes
✓ **Servings:** 4
✓ **Ingredients:**

- 1 eggplant, poked with a fork
- 2 tablespoons tahini paste
- 2 tablespoons lemon juice
- 2 garlic cloves, minced
- 1 tablespoon olive oil
- Salt and black pepper to the taste
- 1 tablespoon parsley, chopped

Directions:

Put the eggplant in a roasting pan, bake at 400 degrees F for 40 minutes, cool down, peel and transfer to your food processor.

Add the rest of the ingredients except the parsley, pulse well, divide into small bowls and serve as an appetizer with the parsley sprinkled on top.

Nutrition: calories 121, fat 4.3, fiber 1, carbs 1.4, protein 4.3

13. Feta Artichoke Dip

✓ **Preparation time:** 10 minutes
✓ **Cooking time:** 30 minutes
✓ **Servings:** 8
✓ **Ingredients:**

- 8 ounces artichoke hearts, drained and quartered
- ¾ cup basil, chopped
- ¾ cup green olives, pitted and chopped
- 1 cup parmesan cheese, grated
- 5 ounces feta cheese, crumbled

Directions:

In your food processor, mix the artichokes with the basil and the rest of the ingredients, pulse well, and transfer to a baking dish.

Introduce in the oven, bake at 375 degrees F for 30 minutes and serve as a party dip.

Nutrition: calories 186, fat 12.4, fiber 0.9, carbs 2.6, protein 1.5

14.   Ginger and Cream Cheese Dip

✓ **Preparation time:** 5 minutes

✓ **Cooking time:** 0 minutes

✓ **Servings:** 6

✓ **Ingredients:**

- ½ cup ginger, grated
- 2 bunches cilantro, chopped
- 3 tablespoons balsamic vinegar
- ½ cup olive oil
- 1 and ½ cups cream cheese, soft

Directions:

In your blender, mix the ginger with the rest of the ingredients and pulse well.

Divide into small bowls and serve as a party dip.

Nutrition: calories 213, fat 4.9, fiber 4.1, carbs 8.8, protein 17.8

15.   Goat Cheese and Chives Spread

✓ **Preparation time:** 10 minutes
✓ **Cooking time:** 0 minutes
✓ **Servings:** 4
✓ **Ingredients:**

- 2 ounces goat cheese, crumbled
- ¾ cup sour cream
- 2 tablespoons chives, chopped
- 1 tablespoon lemon juice
- Salt and black pepper to the taste
- 2 tablespoons extra virgin olive oil

Directions:

In a bowl, mix the goat cheese with the cream and the rest of the ingredients and whisk really well.

Keep in the fridge for 10 minutes and serve as a party spread.

Nutrition: calories 220, fat 11.5, fiber 4.8, carbs 8.9, protein 5.6

16. Herbed Goat Cheese Dip

✓ **Preparation time:** 5 minutes
✓ **Cooking time:** 0 minutes
✓ **Servings:** 4
✓ **Ingredients:**

- ¼ cup mixed parsley, chopped
- ¼ cup chives, chopped
- 8 ounces goat cheese, soft
- Salt and black pepper to the taste
- A drizzle of olive oil

Directions:

In your food processor mix the goat cheese with the parsley and the rest of the ingredients and pulse well.

Divide into small bowls and serve as a party dip.

Nutrition: calories 245, fat 11.3, fiber 4.5, carbs 8.9, protein 11.2

17.   Hummus with Ground Lamb

✓ **Preparation time:** 10 minutes
✓ **Cooking time:** 15 minutes
✓ **Servings:** 8
✓ **Ingredients:**

- 10 ounces hummus
- 12 ounces lamb meat, ground
- ½ cup pomegranate seeds
- ¼ cup parsley, chopped
- 1 tablespoon olive oil
- Pita chips for serving

Directions:

Heat up a pan with the oil over medium-high heat, add the meat, and brown for 15 minutes stirring often.

Spread the hummus on a platter, spread the ground lamb all over, also spread the pomegranate seeds and the parsley and sere with pita chips as a snack.

Nutrition: calories 133, fat 9.7, fiber 1.7, carbs 6.4, protein 5.4

18.   Meatballs Platter

- ✓ **Preparation time:** 10 minutes
- ✓ **Cooking time:** 15 minutes
- ✓ **Servings:** 4
- ✓ **Ingredients:**
    - 1 pound beef meat, ground
    - ¼ cup panko breadcrumbs
    - A pinch of salt and black pepper
    - 3 tablespoons red onion, grated
    - ¼ cup parsley, chopped
    - 2 garlic cloves, minced
    - 2 tablespoons lemon juice
    - Zest of 1 lemon, grated
    - 1 egg
    - ½ teaspoon cumin, ground
    - ½ teaspoon coriander, ground
    - ¼ teaspoon cinnamon powder
    - 2 ounces feta cheese, crumbled
    - Cooking spray

Directions:

In a bowl, mix the beef with the breadcrumbs, salt, pepper and the rest of the ingredients except the cooking spray, stir well and shape medium balls out of this mix.

Arrange the meatballs on a baking sheet lined with parchment paper, grease them with cooking spray and bake at 450 degrees F for 15 minutes.

Arrange the meatballs on a platter and serve as an appetizer.

Nutrition: calories 300, fat 15.4, fiber 6.4, carbs 22.4, protein 35

19. Olives and Cheese Stuffed Tomatoes

✓ **Preparation time:** 10 minutes

✓ **Cooking time:** 0 minutes

✓ **Servings:** 24

✓ **Ingredients:**

- 24 cherry tomatoes, top cut off and insides scooped out
- 2 tablespoons olive oil
- ¼ teaspoon red pepper flakes
- ½ cup feta cheese, crumbled
- 2 tablespoons black olive paste
- ¼ cup mint, torn

Directions:

In a bowl, mix the olives paste with the rest of the ingredients except the cherry tomatoes and whisk well.

Stuff the cherry tomatoes with this mix, arrange them all on a platter and serve as an appetizer.

Nutrition: calories 136, fat 8.6, fiber 4.8, carbs 5.6, protein 5.1

20.   Red Pepper Hummus

✓ **Preparation time:** 10 minutes
✓ **Cooking time:** 0 minutes
✓ **Servings:** 6
✓ **Ingredients:**

- 6 ounces roasted red peppers, peeled and chopped
- 16 ounces canned chickpeas, drained and rinsed
- ¼ cup Greek yogurt
- 3 tablespoons tahini paste
- Juice of 1 lemon
- 3 garlic cloves, minced
- 1 tablespoon olive oil
- A pinch of salt and black pepper
- 1 tablespoon parsley, chopped

Directions:

In your food processor, combine the red peppers with the rest of the ingredients except the oil and the parsley and pulse well.

Add the oil, pulse again, divide into cups, sprinkle the parsley on top and serve as a party spread.

Nutrition: calories 255, fat 11.4, fiber 4.5, carbs 17.4, protein 6.5

21.   Red Pepper Tapenade

✓ **Preparation time:** 10 minutes
✓ **Cooking time:** 0 minutes
✓ **Servings:** 4
✓ **Ingredients:**

- 7 ounces roasted red peppers, chopped
- ½ cup parmesan, grated
- 1/3 cup parsley, chopped
- 14 ounces canned artichokes, drained and chopped
- 3 tablespoons olive oil
- ¼ cup capers, drained
- 1 and ½ tablespoons lemon juice
- 2 garlic cloves, minced

Directions:

In your blender, combine the red peppers with the parmesan and the rest of the ingredients and pulse well.

Divide into cups and serve as a snack.

Nutrition: calories 200, fat 5.6, fiber 4.5, carbs 12.4, protein 4.6

22.   Scallions Dip

✓ **Preparation time:** 5 minutes

✓ **Cooking time:** 0 minutes

✓ **Servings:** 8

✓ **Ingredients:**

- 6 scallions, chopped
- 1 garlic clove, minced
- 3 tablespoons olive oil
- Salt and black pepper to the taste
- 1 tablespoon lemon juice
- 1 and ½ cups cream cheese, soft
- 2 ounces prosciutto, cooked and crumbled

Directions:

In a bowl, mix the scallions with the garlic and the rest of the ingredients except the prosciutto and whisk well.

Divide into bowls, sprinkle the prosciutto on top and serve as a party dip.

Nutrition: calories 144, fat 7.7, fiber 1.4, carbs 6.3, protein 5.5

23. Stuffed Avocado

✓ **Preparation time:** 10 minutes

✓ **Cooking time:** 0 minutes

✓ **Servings:** 2

✓ **Ingredients:**

- 1 avocado, halved and pitted
- 10 ounces canned tuna, drained
- 2 tablespoons sun-dried tomatoes, chopped
- 1 and ½ tablespoon basil pesto
- 2 tablespoons black olives, pitted and chopped
- Salt and black pepper to the taste
- 2 teaspoons pine nuts, toasted and chopped
- 1 tablespoon basil, chopped

Directions:

In a bowl, combine the tuna with the sun-dried tomatoes and the rest of the ingredients except the avocado and stir.

Stuff the avocado halves with the tuna mix and serve as an appetizer.

Nutrition: calories 233, fat 9, fiber 3.5, carbs 11.4, protein 5.6

24.   Tomato Bruschetta

✓ **Preparation time:** 10 minutes
✓ **Cooking time:** 10 minutes
✓ **Servings:** 6
✓ **Ingredients:**

- 1 baguette, sliced
- 1/3 cup basil, chopped
- 6 tomatoes, cubed
- 2 garlic cloves, minced
- A pinch of salt and black pepper
- 1 teaspoon olive oil
- 1 tablespoon balsamic vinegar
- ½ teaspoon garlic powder
- Cooking spray

Directions:

Arrange the baguette slices on a baking sheet lined with parchment paper, grease them with cooking spray and bake at 400 degrees F for 10 minutes.

In a bowl, mix the tomatoes with the basil and the remaining ingredients, toss well and leave aside for 10 minutes.

Divide the tomato mix on each baguette slice, arrange them all on a platter and serve.

Nutrition: calories 162, fat 4 fiber 7, carbs 29, protein 4

25.   Tomato Cream Cheese Spread

✓ **Preparation time:** 5 minutes

✓ **Cooking time:** 0 minutes

✓ **Servings:** 6

✓ **Ingredients:**

- 12 ounces cream cheese, soft
- 1 big tomato, cubed
- ¼ cup homemade mayonnaise
- 2 garlic clove, minced
- 2 tablespoons red onion, chopped
- 2 tablespoons lime juice
- Salt and black pepper to the taste

Directions:

In your blender, mix the cream cheese with the tomato and the rest of the ingredients, pulse well, divide into small cups and serve cold.

Nutrition: calories 204, fat 6.7, fiber 1.4, carbs 7.3, protein 4.5

26.   Tomato Salsa

✓ **Preparation time:** 5 minutes
✓ **Cooking time:** 0 minutes
✓ **Servings:** 6
✓ **Ingredients:**

- 1 garlic clove, minced
- 4 tablespoons olive oil
- 5 tomatoes, cubed
- 1 tablespoon balsamic vinegar
- ¼ cup basil, chopped
- 1 tablespoon parsley, chopped
- 1 tablespoon chives, chopped
- Salt and black pepper to the taste
- Pita chips for serving

Directions:

In a bowl, mix the tomatoes with the garlic and the rest of the ingredients except the pita chips, stir, divide into small cups and serve with the pita chips on the side.

Nutrition: calories 160, fat 13.7, fiber 5.5, carbs 10.1, protein 2.2

27.   Veggie Fritters

✓ **Preparation time:** 10 minutes
✓ **Cooking time:** 10 minutes
✓ **Servings:** 8
✓ **Ingredients:**

- 2 garlic cloves, minced
- 2 yellow onions, chopped
- 4 scallions, chopped
- 2 carrots, grated
- 2 teaspoons cumin, ground
- ½ teaspoon turmeric powder
- Salt and black pepper to the taste
- ¼ teaspoon coriander, ground
- 2 tablespoons parsley, chopped
- ¼ teaspoon lemon juice
- ½ cup almond flour
- 2 beets, peeled and grated
- 2 eggs, whisked
- ¼ cup tapioca flour
- 3 tablespoons olive oil

Directions:

In a bowl, combine the garlic with the onions, scallions and the rest of the ingredients except the oil, stir well and shape medium fritters out of this mix.

Heat up a pan with the oil over medium-high heat, add the fritters, cook for 5 minutes on each side, arrange on a platter and serve.

Nutrition: calories 209, fat 11.2, fiber 3, carbs 4.4, protein 4.8

28.   Walnuts Yogurt Dip

✓ **Preparation time:** 5 minutes

✓ **Cooking time:** 0 minutes

✓ **Servings:** 8

✓ **Ingredients:**

- 3 garlic cloves, minced
- 2 cups Greek yogurt
- ¼ cup dill, chopped
- 1 tablespoon chives, chopped
- ¼ cup walnuts, chopped
- Salt and black pepper to the taste

Directions:

In a bowl, mix the garlic with the yogurt and the rest of the ingredients, whisk well, divide into small cups and serve as a party dip.

Nutrition: calories 200, fat 6.5, fiber 4.6, carbs 15.5, protein 8.4

29.   White Bean Dip

✓ Preparation time: 10 minutes
✓ Cooking time: 0 minutes
✓ Servings: 4
✓ Ingredients:

- 15 ounces canned white beans, drained and rinsed
- 6 ounces canned artichoke hearts, drained and quartered
- 4 garlic cloves, minced
- 1 tablespoon basil, chopped
- 2 tablespoons olive oil
- Juice of ½ lemon
- Zest of ½ lemon, grated
- Salt and black pepper to the taste

Directions:

In your food processor, combine the beans with the artichokes and the rest of the ingredients except the oil and pulse well.

Add the oil gradually, pulse the mix again, divide into cups and serve as a party dip.

Nutrition: calories 274, fat 11.7, fiber 6.5, carbs 18.5, protein 16.5

30.   Wrapped Plums

✓ **Preparation time:** 5 minutes

✓ **Cooking time:** 0 minutes

✓ **Servings:** 8

✓ **Ingredients:**

- 2 ounces prosciutto, cut into 16 pieces
- 4 plums, quartered
- 1 tablespoon chives, chopped
- A pinch of red pepper flakes, crushed

Directions:

Wrap each plum quarter in a prosciutto slice, arrange them all on a platter, sprinkle the chives and pepper flakes all over and serve.

Nutrition: calories 30, fat 1, fiber 0, carbs 4, protein 2

31. Yogurt Dip

✓ **Preparation time:** 10 minutes
✓ **Cooking time:** 0 minutes
✓ **Servings:** 6
✓ **Ingredients:**

- 2 cups Greek yogurt
- 2 tablespoons pistachios, toasted and chopped
- A pinch of salt and white pepper
- 2 tablespoons mint, chopped
- 1 tablespoon kalamata olives, pitted and chopped
- ¼ cup za'atar spice
- ¼ cup pomegranate seeds
- 1/3 cup olive oil

Directions:

In a bowl, combine the yogurt with the pistachios and the rest of the ingredients, whisk well, divide into small cups and serve with pita chips on the side.

Nutrition: calories 294, fat 18, fiber 1, carbs 21, protein 10

32. Apples and Plum Cake

✓ **Preparation Time:** 10 minutes

✓ **Cooking Time:** 40 minutes

✓ **Servings:** 4

✓ **Ingredients:**

- 7 oz. almond flour

- egg, whisked

- 5 tbsps. stevia

- oz. warm almond milk

- pounds plums, pitted and cut into quarters

- 2 apples, cored and chopped

- Zest of 1 lemon, grated

- 1 tsp. baking powder

Directions:

1. In a bowl, mix the almond milk with the egg, stevia, and the rest of the ingredients except the cooking spray and whisk well.

2. Grease a cake pan with the oil, pour the cake mix inside, introduce in the oven, and bake at 350F for 40 minutes.

3. Cool down, slice, and serve.

Nutrition:

Calories 209, Fat: 6.4g, Fiber: 6g, Carbs: 8g, Protein: 6.6g

33. Banana Shake Bowls

✓ **Preparation Time:** 5 minutes

✓ **Cooking Time:** 0 minutes

✓ **Servings:** 4

✓ **Ingredients:**

- 4 medium bananas, peeled

- avocado, peeled, pitted and mashed

- ¾ cup almond milk

- ½ tsp. vanilla extract

Directions:

1. In a blender, combine the bananas with the avocado and the other ingredients, pulse, divide into bowls and keep in the fridge until serving.

Nutrition:

Calories 185, Fat: 4.3g, Fiber: 4g, Carbs: 6g, Protein: 6.45g

34. Blackberry and Apples Cobbler

✓ **Preparation Time:** 10 minutes
✓ **Cooking Time:** 30 minutes
✓ **Servings:** 6
✓ **Ingredients:**

- ¾ cup stevia

- 6 cups blackberries

- ¼ cup apples, cored and cubed

- ¼ tsp. baking powder

- tbsp. lime juice

- ½ cup almond flour

- ½ cup water and ½ tbsp. avocado oil

- Cooking spray

Directions:

1. In a bowl, mix the berries with half of the stevia and lemon juice, sprinkle some flour all over, whisk and pour into a baking dish greased with cooking spray.

2. In another bowl, mix flour with the rest of the sugar, baking powder, the water and the oil, and stir the whole thing with your hands.

3. Spread over the berries, introduce in the oven at 375F and bake for 30 minutes.

4. Serve warm.

Nutrition:

Calories 221, Fat: 6.3g, Fiber: 3.3g, Carbs: 6g, Protein: 9g

35. Black Tea Cake

- ✓ **Preparation Time:** 10 minutes
- ✓ **Cooking Time:** 35 minutes
- ✓ **Servings:** 8
- ✓ **Ingredients:**

  - 6 tbsps. black tea powder

  - 2 cups almond milk, warmed up

  - cup avocado oil

  - cups stevia

  - eggs

  - 2 tsps. vanilla extract

  - ½ cups almond flour

  - 1 tsp. baking soda

  - 3 tsps. baking powder

Directions:

1. In a bowl, combine the almond milk with the oil, stevia and the rest of the ingredients and whisk well.

2. Pour this into a cake pan lined with parchment paper, introduce in the oven at 350F and bake for 35 minutes.

3. Leave the cake to cool down, slice and serve.

Nutrition:

Calories 200, Fat: 6.4g, Fiber: 4g, Carbs: 6.5g, Protein: 5.4g

36. Cherry Cream

- ✓ **Preparation Time:** 2 hours
- ✓ **Cooking Time**: 0 minutes
- ✓ **Servings**: 4
- ✓ **Ingredients:**

  - 2 cups cherries, pitted and chopped

  - cup almond milk

  - ½ cup whipping cream

  - eggs, whisked

  - 1/3 cup stevia

  - 1 tsp. lemon juice

  - ½ tsp. vanilla extract

Directions:

1. In your food processor, combine the cherries with the milk and the rest of the ingredients, pulse well, divide into cups and keep in the fridge for 2 hours before Servings.

Nutrition:

Calories 200, Fat: 4.5g, Fiber: 3.3g, Carbs: 5.6g, Protein: 3.4g

37. Chocolate Baklava

✓ **Preparation Time:** 46 minutes
✓ **Cooking Time:** 35 minutes
✓ **Servings:** 24(1 piece)
✓ **Ingredients:**

- 24 sheets (14 x 9-inch) frozen whole-wheat phyllo (filo) dough, thawed

- 1/8 tsp. salt

- 1/3 cup toasted walnuts, chopped coarsely

- 1/3 cup almonds, blanched toasted, chopped coarsely

- ½ tsp. ground cinnamon

- ½ cup water

- ½ cup hazelnuts, toasted, chopped coarsely

- ½ cup pistachios, roasted, chopped coarsely

- ¾ cup honey

- ½ cup of butter, melted

- cup chocolate-hazelnut spread (I used Nutella)

- 1-piece (3-inch) cinnamon stick

- Cooking spray

Directions:

1. Into medium-sized saucepan, combine the water, honey, and the cinnamon stick; stir until the honey is dissolved. Increase the heat/flame to medium; continue cooking for about 10 minutes without stirring. A candy thermometer should read 230F. Remove the saucepan from the heat and then keep warm. Remove and discard the cinnamon stick.

2. Preheat the oven to 350F.

3. Put the chocolate-hazelnut spread into microwavable bowl; microwave the spread for about 30 seconds on HIGH or until the spread is melted.

4. In a bowl, combine the hazelnuts, pistachios, almonds, walnuts, ground cinnamon, and the salt.

5. Lightly grease with the cooking spray a 9 x 13-inch ceramic or glass baking dish.

6. Put 1 sheet lengthwise into the bottom of the prepared baking dish, extending the ends of the sheet over the edges of the dish. Lightly brush the sheet with the butter. Repeat the process with 5 sheets phyllo and a light brush of butter. Drizzle 1/3 cup of the melted chocolate-hazelnut spread over the buttered phyllo sheets. Sprinkle about 1/3 of the nut mixture (½ cup) over the spread. Repeat the process, layering phyllo sheet, brush of butter, spread, and with nut mixture. For the last, nut mixture top layer, top with 6 phyllo sheets, pressing each phyllo gently into the dish and brushing each sheet with butter.

7. Slice the layers into 24 portions by making 3 cuts lengthwise and then 5 cuts crosswise with a sharp knife; bake for about 35 minutes at 350F or until the phyllo sheets are golden. Remove the dish from the oven, drizzle the honey sauce over the baklava. Pace the dish on a wire rack and let cool. Cover and store the baklavas at normal room temperature if not serving right away.

8. Notes: The sheets of phyllo are delicately thin so handle them with care to avoid tearing them. Cover the sheets with damp cloth so they won't dry out while you are working.

Nutrition:

Calories 238, Fat: 13.4g, Carbs: 27.8g, Fiber: 1.6g, Protein: 4g

38. Cocoa Brownies

✓ **Preparation Time:** 10 minutes
✓ **Cooking Time:** 20 minutes
✓ **Servings:** 8
✓ **Ingredients:**

- 30 oz. canned lentils, rinsed and drained
- tbsp. honey
- 1 banana, peeled and chopped
- ½ tsp. baking soda
- 4 tbsps. almond butter
- tbsps. cocoa powder
- Cooking spray

Directions:

1. In a food processor, combine the lentils with the honey and the other ingredients except the cooking spray and pulse well.

2. Pour this into a pan greased with cooking spray, spread evenly, introduce in the oven at 375F and bake for 20 minutes.

3. Cut the brownies and serve cold.

Nutrition:

Calories 200, Fat: 4.5g, Fiber: 2.4g, Carbs: 8.7g, Protein: 4.3g

39. Cold Lemon Squares

✓ **Preparation Time:** 30 minutes

✓ **Cooking Time:** 0 minutes

✓ **Servings:** 4

✓ **Ingredients:**

- cup avocado oil + a drizzle

- bananas, peeled and chopped

- 1 tbsp. honey

- ¼ cup lemon juice

- A pinch of lemon zest, grated

Directions:

1. In your food processor, mix the bananas with the rest of the ingredients, pulse well and spread on the bottom of a pan greased with a drizzle of oil.

2. Introduce in the fridge for 30 minutes, slice into squares and serve.

Nutrition:

Calories 136, Fat: 11.2g, Fiber: 0.2g, Carbs: 7g, Protein: 1.1g

40. Compote Dipped Berries Mix

✓ **Preparation Time:** 20 minutes

✓ **Servings:** 8

✓ **Ingredients:**

- 2 cups fresh strawberries, hulled and halved lengthwise

- 4 sprigs fresh mint

- 2 cups fresh blackberries

- cup pomegranate juice

- Tsps. vanilla

- 6 orange pekoe tea bags

- cups fresh red raspberries

- 1 cup water

- 2 cups fresh golden raspberries

- 2 cups fresh sweet cherries, pitted and halved

- 2 cups fresh blueberries

- 2 ml bottle Sauvignon Blanc

Directions:

1. Preheat the oven to 290F and lightly grease a baking dish.

2. Soak mint sprigs and tea bags in boiled water for about 10 minutes in a covered bowl.

3. Mix all the berries and cherries in another bowl and keep aside.

4. Cook wine with pomegranate juice in a saucepan and add strained tea liquid.

5. Toss in the mixed berries to serve and enjoy.

Nutrition:

Calories 356, Fat: 0.8g, Carbs: 89.9g, Fiber: 9.4g, Protein: 2.2g

41. Glazed Mediterranean Puffy Fig

✓ **Preparation Time:** 5 minutes

✓ **Cooking Time:** 25 minutes

✓ **Servings:** 8

✓ **Ingredients:**

- 2 sheets (from 1 pack of 4 sheets) puff pastry

- 20 figs or dry figs (dry or fresh)

- 8 oz. mascarpone cheese

- 2 tbsps. butter

- ½ cup (or 8 tbsps.) honey

- ½ tsp. cinnamon

- ½ tsp. nutmeg

- ¼ tsp. salt

- 4 mint leaves, for garnish

Directions:

1. Preheat the oven 400F.

2. Slice the puff pastry into triangle and place into a nonstick baking sheet; bake for about 15-20 minutes or until golden brown. When bakes, remove from the oven and allow to cool.

3. If using dry figs, rehydrate for 1 hour and then cut into half. Put the butter into a nonstick pan over medium flame or heat.

Add the figs; cook for about 3 to 5 minutes. Add the honey, salt, cinnamon, and nutmeg; cook, stirring, for about 3 minutes. Remove the skillet from hat and allow to cool for about 5 to 10 minutes.

4. Place a baked pastry slice in a serving plate, top with 1 tbsp. of cheese, some figs, and then drizzle with the glaze. Repeat the topping, if desired. Garnish with the mint leaves and serve.

Nutrition:

Calories 486, Fat: 22.8g, Carbs: 67.4g, Fiber: 5.4g, Protein: 7.9g

42. Figs Pie

✓ **Preparation Time:** 10 minutes
✓ **Cooking Time:** 1 hour
✓ **Servings:** 8
✓ **Ingredients:**

- ½ cup stevia

- 6 figs, cut into quarters

- ½ tsp. vanilla extract

- cup almond flour

- 4 eggs, whisked

Directions:

1. Spread the figs on the bottom of a spring form pan lined with parchment paper.

2. In a bowl, combine the other ingredients, whisk, and pour over the figs,

3. Bake at 375F for 1 hour, flip the pie upside down when it's done and serve.

Nutrition:

Calories 200, Fat: 4.4g, Fiber: 3g, Carbs: 7.6g, Protein: 8g

43. Greek Cheesecake

✓ **Preparation Time:** 1 hour, 20 minutes

✓ **Cooking Time:** 30 minutes

✓ **Servings:** 8-10

✓ **Ingredients:**

- 4 eggs

- 250g whole-wheat digestive cookies

- 125g butter, melted

- ½ tsp. cinnamon

- ½ cup sugar

- ½ cup honey

- tsp. vanilla extract

- 1 tsp. lemon zest

- 1 kilo white mizithra cheese, fresh or anything similar like ricotta

✓ **For the topping:**

- 750g black cherries, pitted

- 2 leaves gelatin

- 300g sugar

Directions:

1. Process the digestive biscuits in a food processor until crumbled. Add the butter and cinnamon, process again until the mixture is like wet sand in texture. Press the mixture into a 20-cm spring-form tin, pressing some of the mixture up the sides of the tin to make a ridge. Refrigerate until ready to use.

2. Preheat the oven to 180C.

3. With an electric mixer, beat the sugar and the cheese together until creamy. One by one, add in the eggs, the lemon zest, the vanilla extract, and honey. Pour the cheese mixture over the refrigerated biscuit base.

4. Place the spring-form tin in the oven and with the oven door ajar, bake for 30 minutes or until firm. Remove the cake from the oven and let cool.

5. Meanwhile prepare the cherries. Place the gelatin leaves in a bowl with cold water, soak until soft. Put the sugar and the pitted cherries into a frying pan, heat over high flame or hear; stew for about 6 minutes or until the cherries release their juices. Add in the softened gelatins; stir well until well mixed. Remove the pan from the heat and let cool for a bit. When slightly cool, pour over the cooled cheesecake.

6. Refrigerate until the cherry topping set. Serve cold. If desired, serve with vanilla ice cream.

Nutrition:

Calories 561, Fat: 19.9g, Carbs: 80.5g, Fiber: 0.6g, Protein: 18.8g

44. Green Tea and Vanilla Cream

- ✓ **Preparation Time:** 2 hours
- ✓ **Cooking Time:** 0 minutes
- ✓ **Servings:** 4
- ✓ **Ingredients:**

  - 14 oz. almond milk, hot

  - 2 tbsps. green tea powder

  - 14 oz. heavy cream

  - 3 tbsps. stevia

  - tsp. vanilla extract

  - 1 tsp. gelatin powder

Directions:

1. In a bowl, combine the almond milk with the green tea powder and the rest of the ingredients, whisk well, cool down, divide into cups, and keep in the fridge for 2 hours before Servings.

Nutrition:

Calories 120, Fat: 3g, Fiber: 3g, Carbs: 7g, Protein: 4g

45. Hazelnut-Orange Olive Oil Cookies

✓ **Preparation Time:** 30 minutes, plus 1-hour firming

✓ **Cooking Time:** 20 minutes

✓ **Servings**: 6 dozen cookies

✓ **Ingredients:**

- 5 oz. (1 1/8 cups) whole-wheat flour

- 5 oz. (1 1/8 cups) unbleached all-purpose flour

- ¾ cup plus 2 tbsps. granulated sugar

- 2 large eggs

- 2 cups toasted and skinned hazelnuts

- ¼ tsp. table salt

- ½ cup olive oil, extra-virgin

- tsp. vanilla extract, pure

- 1 tsp. of baking powder

- Finely grated zest of 2 medium-sized oranges (about 1 ½ packed tbsp.)

Directions:

1. Put the hazelnuts in a food processor; process until finely ground. In a medium bowl, whisk the ground hazelnuts, flours, baking powder, and salt until blended. With a stand or a hand mixer fitted with a paddle attachment, beat the eggs, oil, sugar, orange zest, and vanilla on LOW speed for about 15 seconds or

until the sugar is moistened. Increase the speed to HIGH; mix for 15 minutes more or until well combined, the sugar will be dissolved at this point. Add the hazelnut mixture; mix on LOW speed for about 30 to 60 seconds or until the dough has just pulled together.

2. Divide the dough into 2 portions. Pile one of the dough's on a piece of parchment paper. With the aid of the parchment paper, shape the dough into a 2-inch diameter 11-inch long log. Wrap the parchment around the log, twisting the ends to secure it. Repeat the process with the remaining dough. Refrigerate and chill for about 1 hour or until firm.

3. Position the oven racks in the lower thirds and the upper position in the oven; preheat the oven to 350F. Line 4 pieces cookie sheets with nonstick baking liners or parchment paper.

4. Unwrap the logs. Cut the logs into ¼ -inch thick slices. Set them 1-inch apart from each other on the prepared sheets. Place 2 baking sheets in the oven; bake the cookies for about 10 minutes or until the cookies are light golden around the edges and on the bottoms, swapping and rotating the sheets halfway through the baking. Let the cookies cool completely on racks. These can be kept in an airtight container at normal room temperature for up to 7 days.

5. Notes: you can make the dough logs ahead of time. Freeze them for up to 1 month.

Nutrition:

Calories 60, Fat: 4g, Carbs: 6g, Fiber: 0g

46. Mediterranean Stuffed Custard Pancakes

- ✓ **Preparation Time:** 60 minutes
- ✓ **Cooking Time:** 20 minutes
- ✓ **Servings:** 10
- ✓ **Ingredients:**
- ✓ **For the batter:**

  - 2 cups flour

  - ½ cup whole-wheat flour

  - 2 cups milk

  - cup water

  - 1 tsp. yeast

  - 1 tsp. baking powder

  - 1 tsp. sugar

- ✓ **For the custard:**

  - cups whole milk

  - cups fat-free milk or 2 % milk

  - 1 cup heavy cream

  - tbsps. sugar

  - ½ cup cornstarch

  - ½ cup water

- 7 pieces medium-sized white bread, crust removed

- 1 tbsp. rose water

- 1 tbsp. orange blossom water

- For the topping:

- 1 cup pistachio

- 1 tbsp. honey or simple syrup

Directions:

For the custard:

1. In a medium-sized pot, pour in the milks, heavy cream, cornstarch, and sugar; heat the mixture, stirring.

2. Cut the bread into pieces and add into the pot; stir until the mixture starts to thicken. Add the orange and rose water; stir until the custard is very thick. Remove from the heat and then pour into a bowl; let cool for 1 hour, stirring every 15 minutes. Cover with saran wrap and then refrigerate to completely cool.

For the batter:

1. Mix all the batter ingredients in a mixing bowl, stirring until well combined; let sit for 20 minutes.

2. Over medium-low flame or heat, heat a nonstick pan. Pour ¼ cup-worth of the batter to make a 3-inch diameter pancake; cook for about 30 seconds or until the top of the batter is bubbly and no longer wet and the bottom is golden brown.

Transfer into a dish to cool. Repeat the process with the remaining batter.

To assemble:

1. Take out the bowl of custard from the refrigerator. Transfer the chilled custard into a piping bag.

2. Fold a pancake together, pinching the edges to make a pocket. Pipe the custard into the pancake pocket, filling it. Repeat the process with the remaining pancakes and custard. Top each filled pocket with the ground pistachio. Refrigerate until ready to serve. To serve, transfer the custard-filled pancakes into a serving plate, drizzle with honey or simple syrup.

Nutrition:

Calories 450, Fat: 19g, Carbs: 60g, Fiber: 2.8g, Protein: 13g

47. Orange-Glazed Fruit and Ouzo Whipped Cream

- ✓ **Preparation Time:** 20 minutes, plus 30 minutes chilling
- ✓ **Cooking Time:** 10 minutes
- ✓ **Servings:** 4
- ✓ **Ingredients:**

  - 3 cups fruit (such as tangerine wedges, quartered apricots or plums, or strips of mango)

  - tbsp. olive oil spread/butter divided (I Can't Believe It's Not Butter! ®), melted

  - Chopped almonds, optional (or pistachios)

- ✓ **For the ouzo whipped cream**:

  - tsp. sugar

  - 1 tsp. ouzo liqueur (anise-flavored), orange juice, orange liqueur, or several drops of anise extract

  - ½ cup whipping cream

- ✓ **For the sauce:**

  - 2 tbsps. sugar

  - 2 tbsps. honey

  - ¼ cup orange juice

Directions:

For the syrup:

1. Mix the syrup ingredients inside a small-sized saucepan. Bring the mixture to a boil, stirring, until the honey and the sugar are dissolved and reduce the heat. Simmer the mixture, without cover, for 10 minutes and set aside.

For the ouzo whipped cream:

1. In a medium-sized chilled bowl, beat the ouzo whipped cream ingredients using electric mixer on medium speed until soft peaks form with the tips curled. Cover and refrigerate for about 30 minutes to chill.

For the grilled fruit:

1. Toss the melted olive oil butter and the fruit in a mixing bowl. Transfer the fruit into a foil pan (see notes) or grill pan.

2. If using charcoal grill, put pan with fruits on the uncovered grill rack over medium coals; grill for about 10-12 minutes, stirring occasionally, until the fruits are heated through.

3. If using gas grill, first, preheat the grill, then reduce to medium heat. Put the grill rack on the grill rack. Cover the grill and grill for about 10-12 minutes, stirring occasionally, until the fruits are heated through.

4. Divide the fruits between 4 pieces dessert plates and drizzle with the honey syrup. If desired, sprinkle with the almonds. Serve with the ouzo whipped cream.

5. Notes: I Can't Believe It's Not Butter! ® is a great butter alternative made with oil blends, water, and salt. It's a simple and delicious spread that's all-natural. To make the foil pan, fold a heavy foil into double thickness. Fold the sides up to create a pan and then cut slits in the bottom.

Nutrition:

Calories 267, Fat: 15g, Carbs: 36g, Fiber: 2g, Protein: 2g

48. Poached Cherries

- ✓ **Preparation Time:** 10 minutes
- ✓ **Cooking Time:** 10 minutes
- ✓ **Servings:** 5 (½ cup each)
- ✓ **Ingredients:**

  - lb. fresh and sweet cherries, rinsed, pitted

  - strips (1 x 3 inches each) orange zest,

  - strips (1 x 3 inches each) lemon zest,

  - 2/3 cup sugar

  - 15 peppercorns

  - ¼ vanilla bean, split but not scraped

  - ¾ cups water

Directions:

1. In a saucepan, mix the water, citrus zest, sugar, peppercorns, and vanilla bean; bring to a boil, stirring until the sugar is dissolved. Add the cherries; simmer for about 10 minutes until the cherries are soft, but not falling apart. Skim any foam from the surface and let the poached cherries cool. Refrigerate with the poaching liquid. Before Servings, strain the cherries.

Nutrition:

Calories 170, Fat: 1g, Carbs: 42g, Fiber: 2g

49. Strawberries Cream

✓ **Preparation Time:** 10 minutes
✓ **Cooking Time:** 20 minutes
✓ **Servings:** 4
✓ **Ingredients:**

- ½ cup stevia

- 2 pounds strawberries, chopped

- cup almond milk

- Zest of 1 lemon, grated

- ½ cup heavy cream

- egg yolks, whisked

Directions:

1. Heat up a pan with the milk over medium-high heat, add the stevia and the rest of the ingredients, whisk well, simmer for 20 minutes, divide into cups and serve cold.

Nutrition:

Calories 152, Fat: 4.4g, Fiber: 5.5g, Carbs: 5.1g, Protein: 0.8g

50. Tiny Orange Cardamom Cookies

- ✓ **Preparation Time:** 48 minutes
- ✓ **Cooking Time:** 12 minutes
- ✓ **Servings:** 80 cookies (5 cookies per Servings)
- ✓ **Ingredients:**

  - ½ cup whole-wheat flour

  - ½ cup all-purpose flour

  - large egg

  - 1 tbsp. sesame seeds, toasted, optional (salted roasted pistachios, chopped)

  - 1 tsp. orange zest

  - 1 tsp. vanilla extract

  - ½ cup butter, softened

  - ½ cup sugar

  - ¼ tsp. ground cardamom

Directions:

1. Preheat the oven to 375F.

2. In a medium bowl, blend the orange zest and the sugar thoroughly, and then blend in the cardamom. Add the butter and with a mixer, beat until the mixture is fluffy and light. Beat

in the egg and the vanilla into the mixture. With the mixer on low speed, mix in the flours into the mixture.

3. Line 3 baking sheets with parchment paper. Using a level tsp. measure, drop batter of the cookie mixture onto the sheets. Top each cookie with a pinch of sesame seeds or nuts, if desired; bake for 1bout 10-12 minutes or until the cookies are brown at the edges and crisp. When baked, transfer the cookies on a cooling rack and let them cool completely.

Nutrition:

Calories 113, Protein: 1.4g, Fat: 6.5g, Carbs: 12g, Fiber: 0.3g

51. Watermelon-Strawberry Rosewater Yogurt Panna Cotta

- ✓ **Preparation Time:** 20 minutes
- ✓ **Cooking Time:** 5 minutes
- ✓ **Servings:** 4
- ✓ **Ingredients:**

  - 500 g seedless watermelon, peeled, and cut into 5-mm pieces

  - 3 tsps. rosewater

  - 250 ml honey-flavored yogurt

  - 250 ml (1 cup) thickened cream

  - 2 tsps. gelatin powder

  - 2 tbsps. caster sugar

  - 10 strawberries, washed, hulled, and cut into 5-mm pieces

  - tbsp. hot water

  - Honey, to serve

  - Vegetable oil, to grease

Directions:

1. Brush 4 pieces of 125 ml or ½ cup sprinkle molds with vegetable oil to grease.

2. Put the yogurt into a large-sized heat-safe bowl.

3. Place the sugar and the cream into a small-sized saucepan and heat over medium heat; stir until the sugar is heated through and the sugar is dissolved.

4. Place the hot water into a small-sized heat-safe bowl. Sprinkle the gelatin over the hot water. Place the bowl into a small-sized saucepan. Add enough boiling water to fill the saucepan about ¾ deep on the side of the bowl. With a fork, whisk the mixture until the gelatin is dissolved.

5. Add the gelatin mixture and the cream mixture into the yogurt, whisking until well combined. Strain the mixture through a fine sieve over a large-sized jug. Pour the strained mixture into the prepared molds. Cover each mold with a plastic wrap. Refrigerate for at least 6 hours or overnight until set.

6. In a medium bowl, combine the strawberry, watermelon, and rosewater.

7. Turn the panna cottas into Servings bowl. Spoon the strawberry-watermelon over each panna cotta. Drizzle with honey and serve.

8. Notes: For a different version, you can omit the rosewater, strawberries, and the honey. Combine the watermelon with 1/3 cup of fresh passion fruit pulp, and spoon over the panna cottas.

Nutrition:

Calories 364.96, Fat: 26g, Carbs: 26g, Fiber: 1g, Protein: 7g